MINECRAFT ZONE

« MINECRAFT »
MAPS

UNOFFICIAL GAMER GUIDE

Zelda Wagner

Lerner Publications ◆ Minneapolis

Lerner Publications Company
An imprint of Lerner Publishing Group, Inc.
241 First Avenue North
Minneapolis, MN 55401 USA

For reading levels and more information, look up this title at www.lernerbooks.com.

Main body text set in ITC Franklin Gothic Std.
Typeface provided by Adobe Systems.

Editor: Annie Zheng **Designer:** Mary Ross **Photo Editor:** Angel Kidd
Lerner team: Martha Kranes

Library of Congress Cataloging-in-Publication Data

Names: Wagner, Zelda, 2000– author.
Title: Minecraft maps : unofficial gamer guide / Zelda Wagner.
Description: Minneapolis : Lerner Publications, 2025. | Series: UpDog books.
    Minecraft zone | Includes bibliographical references and index. | Audience: Ages
    8–11 | Audience: Grades 2–3 | Summary: "Maps aren't just for finding your way
    back home; they're for exploring! Readers will enjoy learning about where to
    find maps, how to use them, and even how to create their own in Minecraft"—
    Provided by publisher.
Identifiers: LCCN 2023034513 (print) | LCCN 2023034514 (ebook) | ISBN
    9798765626511 (library binding) | ISBN 9798765629055 (paperback) | ISBN
    9798765635520 (epub)
Subjects: LCSH: Minecraft (Game)—Juvenile literature. | Maps—Juvenile literature.
    | Map reading—Juvenile literature.
Classification: LCC GV1469.35.M535 W3425 2025 (print) | LCC GV1469.35.
    M535 (ebook) | DDC 794.8—dc23/eng/20230831

LC record available at https://lccn.loc.gov/2023034513
LC ebook record available at https://lccn.loc.gov/2023034514

Manufactured in the United States of America
1-1010172-51985-11/15/2023

TABLE OF CONTENTS

LOST AND FOUND

In *Minecraft*, it's easy to get lost. A map can help players find their way.

Players can mark
places on maps.

Maps can also be used to see where a player's friends are.

Best of all, they help
a player return home.

« UP NEXT! »

GETTING A MAP.

MAPMAKER

An explorer map is a special map. It can help lead players to mansions, monuments, and buried treasure.

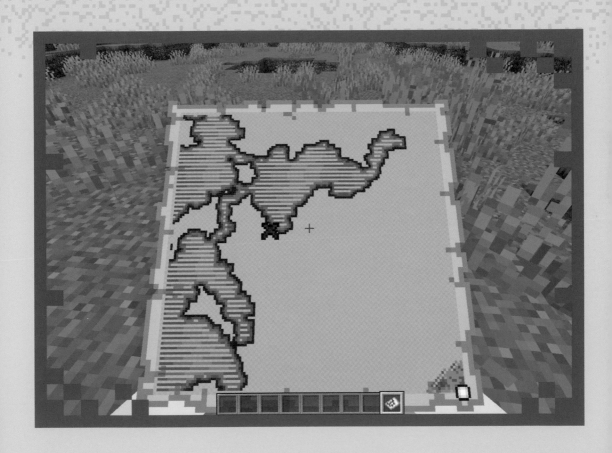

At first, it looks like
an old brown map.

Colors fill the map as
players explore their world.

Players can get explorer maps in villages.

Or players can find maps underwater, such as in a ruin or shipwreck.

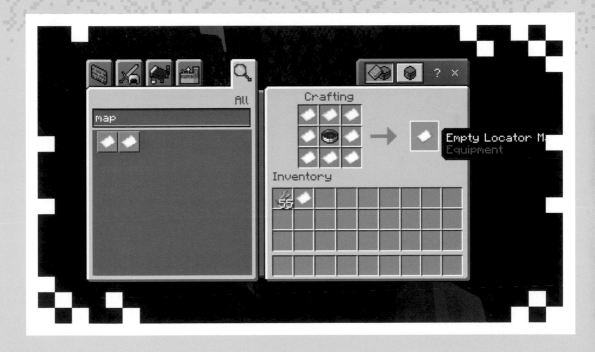

Players can even create their own maps.

≪ GAME ≫
BREAK!

In *Minecraft*, there's so much to explore! Here are some structures players can mark on a map:

1.   Village

2.   Pillager outpost

3.   Monster room

4.   Mineshaft

5.   Ancient city

« **UP NEXT!** »

FILLING a MaP.

all over the map

Maps start out blank.

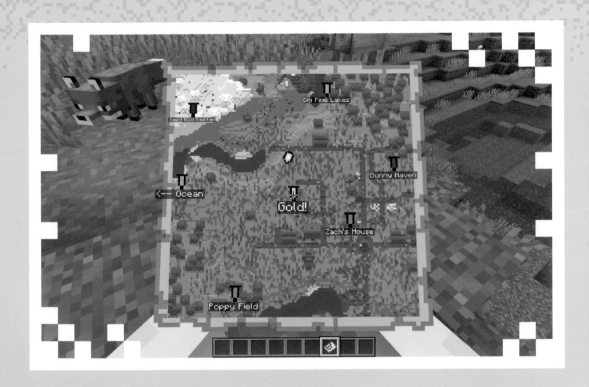

A finished map is filled with colors, symbols, and landmarks.

To complete a map, players
need to explore.

Players move through the world while staying within the map's borders.

The map draws itself
as players explore.

On the computer, players can mark locations by adding waypoints.

Waypoints can be made by planting a banner in the ground and clicking on it with the map.

banner

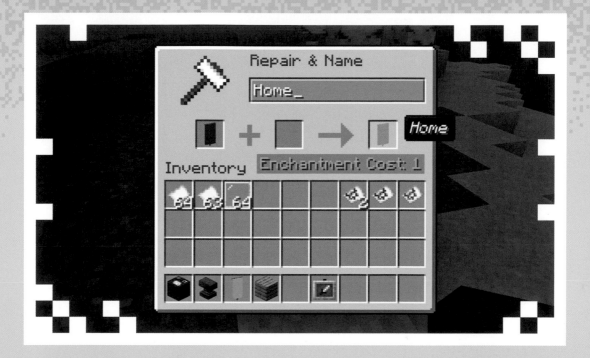

Players can label banners by adding words with an anvil.

« UP NEXT! »

NEW ADVENTURES.

MAP MASTERS

Maps can have levels 0 to 4.

Level 0   Level 1   Level 2   Level 3   Level 4

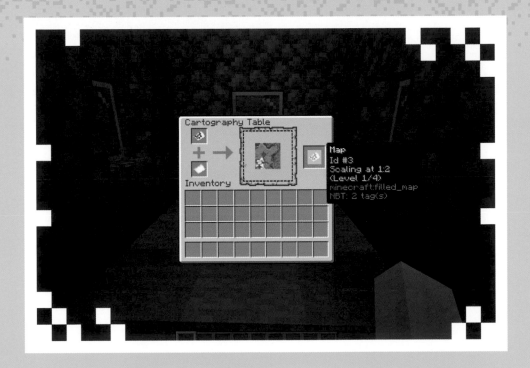

The higher the level, the
more area a map covers.

Maps can be
copied or locked.

A player with a copied map will have a backup in case it's lost.

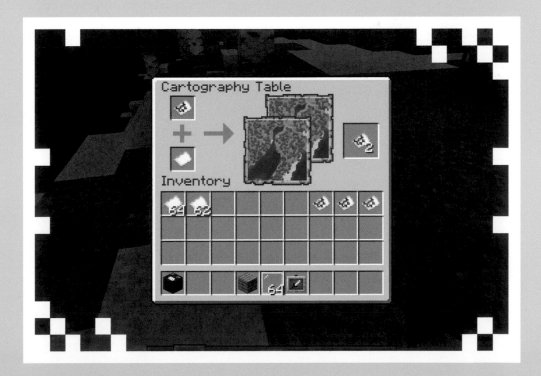

A player with a locked map can't change it if the world changes.

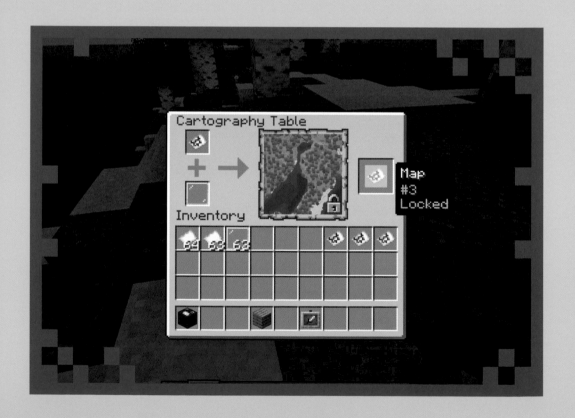

In *Minecraft*, there's always more to explore!

Glossary

anvil: an iron tool

banner: a long strip of cloth

landmark: an object or feature of the land that is easily recognized from a distance

waypoint: a map marker

Check It Out!

Britannica Kids: *Minecraft*
https://kids.britannica.com/students/article/
Minecraft/631450

Kiddle: *Minecraft* Facts for Kids
https://kids.kiddle.co/Minecraft

Koestler-Grack, Rachel A. *Curious about* Minecraft.
Mankato, MN: Amicus, 2024.

Miller, Marie-Therese. *34 Amazing Facts about* Minecraft.
Minneapolis: Lerner Publications, 2024.

Minecraft: How to *Minecraft*
https://www.minecraft.net/en-us/article/how-minecraft

Wagner, Zelda. Minecraft *Mining: Unofficial Gamer Guide*.
Minneapolis: Lerner Publications, 2025.

Index

Photo Acknowledgments

Image credits: Various screenshots by Angel Kidd, Heather Schwartz, Julia Zajac, and Linda Zajac.

Design elements: Anatolii Poliashenko/Getty Images; filo/Getty Images.